Santa Fe
with Kids
from
A to Z

Santa Fe
with Kids
from
A to Z

by
Mary Catherine Mathews
and
Kelsey Daly

Top Things to See
Top Things to Do
Top Day Trips
Top Museums

Plus Kid-friendly Restaurants
and
An Annual Calendar of Not-to-Miss Events

Illustrations by Bob Eggers

SUNSTONE
PRESS

SANTA FE

Sunstone books may be purchased for educational, business, or sales promotional use.
For information please write: Special Markets Department, Sunstone Press,
P.O. Box 2321, Santa Fe, New Mexico 87504-2321.

Library of Congress Cataloging-in-Publication Data:

Mathews, Mary Catherine, 1961–
    Santa Fe with kids from A to Z : top things to see, top things to do, top day trips,
museums, plus kid-friendly restaurants and an annual calendar of not-to-miss events / by
Mary Catherine Mathews and Kelsey Daly.
        p. cm.
    Includes bibliographical references and index.
    ISBN 0-86534-457-4 (softcover : alk. paper)
1. Santa Fe (N.M.)—Guidebooks. 2. Family recreation—New Mexico—Santa Fe—
Guidebooks. 3. Children—Travel—New Mexico—Santa Fe—Guidebooks.
I. Daly, Kelsey, 1964- II. Title.

F804.S23M38 2005
917.89'5604—dc22

                                    2005004176

WWW.SUNSTONEPRESS.COM
SUNSTONE PRESS / POST OFFICE BOX 2321 / SANTA FE, NM 87504-2321 /USA
(505) 988-4418 / *ORDERS ONLY* (800) 243-5644 / FAX (505) 988-1025

CONTENTS

From A to Z

Audubon Center (Randall Davey) / 12

Bandelier National Monument / 14
Bataan Memorial Military Museum / 16
Bicentennial Park and
Swimming Pool / 18
Biking / 20
Bus Tours / 22

Canyon Road / 24
Cerrillos / 26
Cross of the Martyrs / 28

Dinosaurs and More / 30

Eight Northern Pueblos / 32
El Rancho de las Golandrinas / 34

Farmers Market / 36
Fishing / 38

Genoveva Chavez
Community Center / 40
Georgia O'Keeffe Museum / 42

Hiking / 44
Horseback Riding / 46

Restaurants

INTRODUCTION

A trip to Santa Fe can be fun for the entire family. It is truly one of the unique cities of the world dating back to the 1600s. With stunning mountain views and rich culture, there is something for people of all ages. Outdoor activities? Santa Fe has it all. Museums? You're in luck. The hidden treasures in the City Different can be found at every turn. You just have to know where to look. This guide will help you negotiate the winding roads and narrow passages. We want everyone to experience the wonderful world of Santa Fe, especially families with children.

The book is organized in alphabetical order so that you can easily locate places. Each listing includes addresses, phone numbers, websites when available, hours of operation, admission prices and appropriate age ranges. There are also indexes in the front of the book with the top things to do, things to see, day trips and museums. These are the places and things we feel visitors should not miss. Give the kids some crayons or colored pencils and let them color in the illustrations throughout the book.

Following the alphabetical listings is an entire section of kid-friendly restaurants. Don't let the crayons and kids menus fool you, these places have some of the best food and drinks in Santa Fe—not only for junior, but for parents and grandparents too.

Finally, don't miss the Annual Calendar of Events. This will be helpful if you're visiting Santa Fe during a specific season. So read on and plan your trip, your kids will thank you.

We hope you enjoy Santa Fe as much as we do.

Kelsey Daly

Mary Catherine Mathews

Audubon Center
(Randall Davey)

1800 Upper Canyon Road
(505) 983-4609
Adults $2/Children $1
Trails Open During Daylight Hours
Nature Store Daily 9 AM-4 PM
www.newmexicoaudubon.org

Hiking anyone? Bird watching? How about a healthy dose of nature in a beautiful setting? These are just a few of the things in store for you when you visit the Randall Davey Audubon Center. This is one of the true treasures of Santa Fe and you won't want to miss it.

First, getting there. Drive East on Alameda Street, turn left on Upper Canyon Road and keep going, the pavement will give way to a dirt road. You will eventually dead end into the Center. Once you get there, check into the visitors center for information about the walking trails and creatures you might encounter along the way. We spotted horned lizards and several hummingbirds.

As for hiking, there are two trails. Both are perfect for even the youngest hikers. The main loop is half a mile long and is clearly marked…no chance of getting lost. There are benches along the way where you can sit and rest, have a snack or just enjoy the scenery. Veering off the main loop is Bear Canyon. It's a bit steeper, but by no means difficult. The day we went, our youngest hiker was a 4-year-old and had no trouble whatsoever. I was glad that we applied plenty of sunscreen and were wearing hats because there's not a lot of shade. After the hike, stop in at the Nature Store. They have an array of books, pamphlets, gifts and various other souvenirs. Also, be sure to walk over to the historic home and studio of artist Randall Davey. When he died in

1964, he donated his house (a former sawmill) and property (135 acres) to the Audubon Center. Tours of his home are held every Monday at 2:00. The tours are best for older children. The tiny cemetery on the side of the front yard where Davey, his wife and infant daughter are buried is also interesting.

Fun fact:

In the summer, the Randall Davey Audubon Center offers wildly popular day camps. You must sign up months in advance. If you're interested, contact the center in the fall or winter.

A roadrunner : The New Mexico state bird.

Bandelier National Monument

NM State Road 4, 48 miles NW of Santa Fe
(505) 672-0343
$10 per Car
Open Daily Except December 25 and January 1
Summer 8 AM-6 PM
Winter 8 AM-4:30 PM
Spring and Fall 9 AM-5:30 PM
www.nps.gov/band

Bandelier National Monument is the perfect place to show your kids how ancestors of the modern pueblo peoples (early Native Americans) lived. The area was likely inhabited for about 500 years from the 1100s to the late 1500s. Wonderful evidence of the people who lived here has been left in an area that is easy for kids to comprehend and explore.

The Visitor's Center is a great first stop to stock up on books, trail guides and information. Also, there is a short video on the history of the area to get you started. From the Center there is a 1.2-mile Main Loop Trail that will take you through several excavated and restored sites within Frijoles Canyon. You will encounter kivas, which were used for social and religious gatherings, and a circle of pueblo-style buildings that was once the village of Tyounyi. Continuing north along the loop, cave dwellings can be seen along the canyon walls, including the 800 foot long apartment-like Long House.

If you are still feeling adventurous (and we really suggest that you muster the strength) travel the additional half mile from the end of the Main Loop to the Alcove House. You will be rewarded with a restored kiva 140 feet above the floor of the canyon. The kids will love climbing the series of ladders to reach the kiva and enjoy an incredible view of Frijoles Canyon.

After your long trek, stop in at the snack bar. Sample the green chile cheese burgers and the chile cheese fries. Also, don't miss the gift shop, always a hit.

If you have more time and haven't exhausted everyone, Bandelier has more than 70 miles of backcountry hiking trails. Pick up a map at the Visitor's Center and hit the trail.

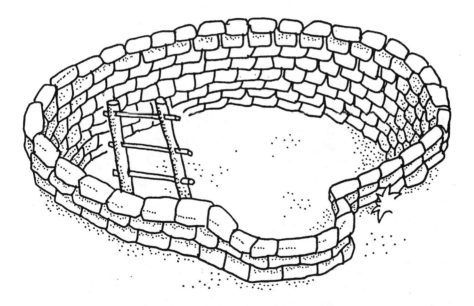

Tip:
The Bradbury Science Museum in Los Alamos
is a great stop on the way home.
Check out the web page for driving directions and information
http://www.lanl.gov/museum.

Bataan Memorial Museum

1050 Old Pecos Trail
(505) 474-1670
Admission is Free
Tuesday, Wednesday, Friday 9 AM-4 PM
Saturday 9 AM-1 PM

Walk through the doors of this former New Mexico National Guard armory and you will find four centuries of military history. The museum is named after the infamous Bataan death march in the Philippines in 1942. When the Americans surrendered to the Japanese in this World War II battle, more soldiers from New Mexico were captured than from any other state. Half of the 1800 young New Mexicans died in that brutal march toward POW camps. Many more died after returning home.

The museum itself is a fascinating history lesson. You'll see photos of soldiers from World War I, World War II, the Korean War, Vietnam and Desert Storm. There are weapons, uniforms and heartbreaking letters. Sit in the museum's library and read up on our country's fight for freedom. Outside the museum, there are tanks which children are occasionally allowed to climb. Bottom line: a wonderful tribute to those who fought for our country. Those interested in military history will be fascinated. Rick, the museum director is a former military history teacher. He's a wealth of knowledge and says this museum is best for children eight years old and over. He says younger than that and they usually don't understand what "war" is.

Tip:
Call the museum before showing up.
There's only one employee and if he's gone, the museum is closed.

Bicentennial Park and Swimming Pool

1121 Alto Street
(505) 955-4779
Adults $1.85/Children $.75
Pool is open from Memorial Day
through Late September

This is a great stop for some family fun in Santa Fe. You can see the two outdoor swimming pools and colorful playground from West Alameda Street. The playground is best for young children- under the age of four or five. There are lots of small, bright climbing structures, a seesaw and plenty of places to run around and exercise those little legs. Next to the playground is the only public outdoor pool in Santa Fe. Actually, there are two pools. The tot pool is an oasis for kids under 7. They splash around in shallow water while parents sit and watch… or splash along with them. The little ones flock to the frog slide and to the waterfall, which is shaped like a big mushroom. Adjacent to the tot pool is an eight-lane, heated Olympic size pool. Older kids and adults swim, splash or shoot down the double-barreled red slide. In the summer, the pool is open from 6am-9am for lap swimmers. It's fabulous to swim at daybreak with the mountains in the background. Later in the day, the lane ropes come down and the pool opens to the public. It's a bargain, too.

Tip:
There are 2-hour sessions at the pool.
The lifeguards clear the pool after each session and you must pay again for the next session. So, if a session is from 3:15-5:15 and you show up at 5:00, you only get to swim for 15 minutes. It's like this at all the city pools. They also limit the number of people in the pool. So, on a blazing hot summer day... call first to find out session times and whether the pools are crowded (they usually aren't filled to capacity)

Fun Fact:
There's a paved running/biking path, tennis courts, a basketball court and barbecue pits in this shady park.

Biking

Santa Fe has miles and miles of biking trails through the city, across desert terrain and through forests. It is a great way to see parts of the area you would not have the chance to see otherwise. There are trails for beginners to advanced so pick your spot, strap on your helmet and GO. Below are two outfitters to help get you on your way.

Sun Mountain Bike Company
102 East Water Street (in El Centro)
(505) 982-8986
www.sunmountainbikeco.com

Bike N' Sport
524 Suite C. Cordova Road
(505) 820-0809
www.nmbikensport.com

Tip:

Bikers beware. Streets in Santa Fe are narrow and sometimes winding.
Take extra precaution or better yet stick to the trails and bike paths.

Bus Tours

The Loretto Line
Buy your tickets in front of the Loretto Chapel
(505) 983-3701
Adults $14/Kids Under 12 $10 (with parent)
May—October 10 AM-4PM

Santa Fe Detours
(800) Detours or (505) 983-6565
$30 per person
Year-Round

A bus tour is one of the best ways to learn about Santa Fe. Even locals pick up bits of information they didn't know. It's very enjoyable, too. Sit in an open-air trolley and wind through town learning about the oldest capitol city in the United States. The tour guides are knowledgeable and tell about historical areas, Canyon Road, museums and residential neighborhoods. The tours are not cheap, but in our opinion they are worth it. A warning though, this is not for young children. We put the minimum age for this hour and fifteen minute tour at eight years old. Why? Because there's lot of information to absorb and you must be able to sit quietly. The other people on the tram won't appreciate a fussy child. And it gets chilly in the open-air bus. The brochure for the Loretto Line spells it out "young children will hate this tour". Fortunately, our eight-year old visitor loved it, but once he asked "how much longer?" Best bet: bring older children who are interested in learning about Santa Fe.

Tip:
Bring a camera and water bottle. For open air bus rides, bring a jacket.
It gets breezy and cool even on summer days.

Canyon Road

Paseo de Peralta to Palace Avenue

If you're a visitor to Santa Fe you will eventually find yourself on Canyon Road, considered the "Art and Soul of Santa Fe". It has the greatest concentration of art in the city. With more than seventy galleries in a three-quarter of a mile stretch, you can see an incredible range of art! Many of the galleries include sculpture gardens and folk art. Stop by 619 Canyon Road and you can explore an outdoor sculpture garden. If you are lucky you may even see the artist working outside. Across the street check out Off the Wall Gallery at 616 Canyon Road. They have a huge collection of whimsical clocks of all shapes and sizes hanging on the walls. In the back there is a coffee bar with baked goods and a cute outdoor patio in the back - a nice break from your exploring. Next door and down Painter's Alley is the David Ross Studio. The artist makes benches, stools, chairs and doorstops in the form of any breed of dog. He also makes cats, pigs, sheep and even cheetahs. Further up Canyon Road is Houshang's Gallery at 713 Canyon Road where you can find art by Frederick Prescott. He makes large, brightly painted metal sculpture with moving parts. You might see the Lone Ranger riding off into the sunset or a couple in a pink Cadillac driving down Route 66 or even a New York scene with King Kong on top of the Empire State Building.

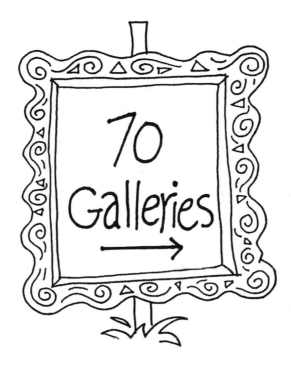

Tip:

Encourage your kids to explore the galleries and pick out the type of art that interests them. After an afternoon of gallery hoping stop by The Painted Dish (page 64) and see if your kids have been inspired to create their own works of art.

Cerrillos

19 Miles South of Santa Fe on Highway 14

A trip to Cerrillos is sure to capture your children's imagination. The tree covered hills have been mined for turquoise by Native Americans, Spanish Colonialists, Mexicans and Territorialists for over a thousand years. As recently as 1983 robbers made off with $500,000 worth of gold from the nearby Ortiz mines! The town was the backdrop for the 1988 movie Young Guns.

Turn right off of Highway 14 at the sign for Cerrillos and explore what is left of the mining town. A stop at Casa Grande Trading Post, Petting Zoo and Mining Museum at the end of the Main Street is a must. Spend a dollar for a bag of food and you can feed the llamas, goats, chickens, doves and various other animals. Next, stop into the trading post where your kids could spend hours pouring over the minerals, rocks, gemstones, rattlesnake skin, petrified wood, old letters, porcupine quills, and various other interesting tidbits. You may not be able to drag them out of there.

Side Trip Tip:

Check out the Broken Saddle Riding Company in town for a horseback riding trip to really get a sense of the area. See page 46 for the details.

Cross of the Martyrs

Paseo de Peralta East of Marcy Street

In Santa Fe it seems all paths lead to Paseo de Peralta. If you're driving on this busy road just east of The Plaza, you'll notice a large white cross on a hill overlooking the city and winding steps leading up to the cross. Do more than just look from your car, pull over and take your children on a quick, educational hike. Along the path, there are plaques telling about Santa Fe's history. You'll find out that Santa Fe is the oldest capital city in the United States dating back to the early 1600s. You'll also find out when and how New Mexico became a state and about the three cultures that make up Santa Fe: the Native Americans, Hispanics and Anglo-Americans. These historical tidbits will be interesting to older children and to adults. Little kids simply enjoy running up the winding brick path and seeing the beautiful views. At the top is the Cross of the Martyrs. It memorializes 21 Franciscan priests and friars killed in the 1680 Pueblo Revolt. The Franciscans successfully helped the Native Americans drive out the Spanish forces. All their names are listed on a plaque underneath the cross. This is a quick, easy and educational adventure suitable for all ages.

Fun Fact:
Take a peek behind the hill, beyond the cross and you'll see Old Fort
Marcy park. Occasionally you'll see llamas roaming near here.

Dinosaurs and More

102 West San Francisco Street (Upstairs)
(505) 988-3299
Free
Open 7 Days, 10 AM-5 PM
www.meteoritefossilgallery.com

Billed as a meteorite, mineral and fossil gallery, Dinosaurs and More seems more like a small natural history museum. The owner, Charlie Snell, who calls himself a self-taught paleontologist and prospector, travels throughout the United States and around the world looking for minerals and meteorites and excavating bones for his shop. He hopes to eventually gather enough material to open a real museum for kids in Santa Fe.

The shop has baskets, buckets, and glass cases filled with treasures from around the globe. You will see quartz from Brazil, cats eye from Morocco, pyrite from Spain and much more. If you need an education on minerals you can study the Minerals of the World chart on the wall.

There are meteorites that have been found everywhere from New Mexico to Australia. One in particular is a "Sudbury" that is 1.87 billion years old and was found in Canada. There are fossils of insects, fish, plants, and coral.

If you like dinosaurs you can choose from a basket of bones from South Dakota that are 65 million years old. If you ask, Charlie will show you cases of t-rex teeth, triceratops horns, a cast of the bones of saber-tooth tiger cubs or a fossilized tail from a car-sized prehistoric cousin of the armadillo called a glyptodon.

Tip:
Charlie is a wealth of information and is happy to spend time with kids
explaining his excavations, sharing information they are interested in or
pulling out special items from behind the counter.

Eight Northern Pueblos

Native American culture, history and art are a major part of Santa Fe and of northern New Mexico. A visit to the region would not be complete without a visit to one or more of the many pueblos in the area. The Eight Northern Pueblos, which include San Ildefonso, Nambe, Picuris, Pojaque, Santa Clara, San Juan, Taos and Tesuque, are an excellent representation of these pueblos and are all within easy driving distance of Santa Fe. Throughout the year there are feast days, dances and other events, which the public are welcome to attend. Many of the dances and festivals are listed in the Annual Calendar of Events on page 112. The Indian Pueblo Cultural Center in Albuquerque is a great place to get information on current events.

Indian Pueblo Cultural Center
(800) 766-4405
www.indianpueblo.org

Tip:
Although the public is welcome to attend many of the dances and celebrations, make sure your family respects the traditions and tone of the day and acts accordingly. Make sure you ask permission before taking photographs.

El Rancho de las Golondrinas

334 Los Pinos Road (15 miles south of Santa Fe)
(505) 471-2261
Adults $5 (Slightly Higher for Festivals)
Seniors and Children 13–18 $4
Children 5–12 $2
June through September
Wednesday—Sunday 10am-4pm
www.golondrinas.org

Want to go back in time and show your kids how people lived in New Mexico in the 18th and 19th centuries? Well this is the place.

El Rancho de las Golondrinas was originally a stopping place along the Camino Real from Mexico City to Santa Fe during the 1700s. In 1932 the Curtin-Paloheimo family acquired the 200-acre property and restored the historic buildings, built authentic structures on old foundations and brought other buildings to the Ranch from other sites. The ranch now houses an 18th century house, a 19th century house and outbuildings, a molasses mill, a threshing ground, water mills, a blacksmith shop, a winery and more. The village portrays living and working conditions of Spanish Colonial and Territorial New Mexico. There is so much to explore at the ranch, everyone will find something to interest them.

In addition, on any given weekend there may be a festival or theme weekend with more activities for you and the kids. You may find yourself watching reenactments of the Civil War in New Mexico, joining in the Spring, Summer or Harvest festivals, partaking in the wine festival, or witnessing the "Lawmen and Desperados" as they were in early New Mexico.

Drinking water and limited food are available at the Ranch. Plan to pack a picnic lunch and find a spot where you can imagine yourself in another century. Of course, there is a fabulous gift shop with something for everyone.

Tip:
Of particular note for those pre-teen girls, the American Girl Doll Josephina was born and raised at the Ranch. You can even arrange for a special "Josephina Tour"—don't forget your doll.

Farmers Market

Summer (April through October)

Corner of Guadalupe Street and Cerrillos Road
(505) 983-4098
Saturdays and Tuesdays
7 AM-12 Noon

Rodeo Grounds
Thursdays 3 PM-7 PM

Winter (November through March)

El Museo Cultural
1614B Paseo de Peralta
Saturdays
9 AM-1 PM
www.farmersmarketsnm.org

This is the place to be in Santa Fe on a spring, summer or fall Saturday or Tuesday morning. It is one of the oldest, largest and most successful farmer's markets in the country. What we like is that it's fun and fresh and absolutely beautiful. Farmers from all over Northern New Mexico bring their food, flowers and special lotions and potions and set up shop. Locals and visitors alike turn out in droves to buy berries, watermelons, cantaloupes, tamales, roasted chiles, baked goods, fresh flowers, herbs and hundreds of other home grown products. The colors and flavors are spectacular. Never have we tasted sweeter blackberries. For children, it's a lesson in farming and commerce. How about giving your child a few dollars to buy flowers or fresh fruit? Strolling through the booths is definitely entertaining and educational. Did we mention there's also live music? Also...there are various events throughout the season. The Lavender Festival in July sounds like fun. Bottom line: a mouth-watering adventure that promotes small farms. Show up early for the best selection of goods and to beat the crowds. It does get busy.

Fun Fact:

A nationally syndicated newspaper recently ranked the Santa Fe Farmers Market one of the best in the nation.

Fishing

The Reel Life
Sanbusco Center (500 Montezuma Avenue)
(505) 995-8114
(877) 733-5543
www.reellifesantafe.com

Only 45 minutes away from Santa Fe is some of the best fly fishing in the area. The Pecos River offers a great place to start your fishing career or to add to it. A little farther and you could be fishing on the Jemez River, Rio San Antonio, Rio Guadalupe or even the Rio Grande. Lake fishing is also an option on nearby Cochiti Lake or an hour north on Abiqui Lake. The Reel Life offers guided trips, classes, and instruction, as well as all the gear you will need to fulfill you and your kid's dreams of catching that huge rainbow trout. They offer classes specifically for kids so they can start out on the right foot and develop a lifelong love of the sport.

Tip:
This is some of the best fly-fishing in the country. If you love the sport don't miss the chance to cast your flies here.

Genoveva Chavez Community Center

3221 Rodeo Road
(505) 955-4000 (info line)
(505) 955-4046 (front desk)
Adults $4
Children 11–17 $1/10 and Under $1
Monday—Friday 6 AM-10 PM
Saturday 8 AM-10 PM
Sunday 10 AM-6 PM
www.chavezcenter.com

The first thing you'll notice about the Chavez Center is what a beautiful facility it is. The place is vast with more to do than you can imagine… both for kids and adults. Kids first.. The children's swimming pool, called the leisure pool, is huge… complete with a swirling river current, a small slide for toddlers and a huge, winding water slide for children 40 inches or taller. The pool can be hectic and crowded, but that doesn't seem to faze the children. Next to the leisure pool is a state of the art lap swimming pool that is 50 meters in length and 25 meters in width. Both pools are indoor so they are open year round.

If parents want to swim laps or work out (there are yoga classes, spinning classes, treadmills, stair masters, a weight room, etc) drop the kids off at the Playzone… a spotless babysitting facility at the Chavez Center. It costs only $2.00 per hour per child.

The center also has a year-round ice skating rink, racquetball courts, a café and more. Call for a schedule of activities or just show up. It's worth a trip. Good for all ages.

Tip:
The dressing rooms are freezing.
Bring plenty of towels and warm clothes for your kids.

Georgia O'Keeffe Museum

217 Johnson Street
(505) 995-0785
Adults $8/Children Under 16 Free
10 AM-5 PM daily
Fridays 5 PM-8 PM free
www.okeeffemuseum.org

Georgia O'Keeffe is a legend in New Mexico and a stop at the O'Keeffe Museum should be on everyone's to-do list while visiting Santa Fe. Her life story is fascinating and her art remarkable. You will learn about O'Keeffe the person, the artist and the special bond she had with New Mexico. There is a very interesting video about O'Keeffe that runs periodically in one of the museum's nine galleries. The video is narrated by actor (and Santa Fe resident) Gene Hackman and is probably best for older children (there is some discussion about the sexual overtones in some of her paintings). In fact, this museum is probably best for children over eight years old.

All ages will enjoy the museum's Fun Family Program. The programs take place one Saturday morning every month. You will have a brief tour of the museum before it opens to the public and then do art projects using clay, glue, wood and other materials. Call for information about the programs. Reservations suggested.

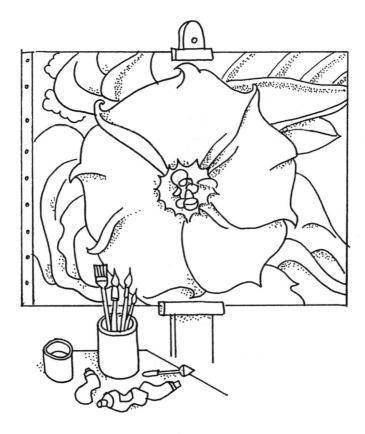

Tip:
Next door to the museum is the O'Keeffe Café,
an upscale place for lunch, dinner or a special dessert.

Hiking

Hiking is a way of life in Santa Fe—what a great way to explore the area. There are trail heads right on the edge of town or you can drive a little farther in most directions to get a little deeper into nature. Even the littlest legs can find a path that will suit their abilities.

The Atalaya Trail is a strenuous 3-mile hike up to the top of Atalaya Mountain and back. A hearty 6-year old can definitely make the trip and it is worth it for the beautiful view of Santa Fe you get from the top. To get to the trail head take Camino del Monte Sol south from downtown and turn left on Camino Cruz Blanca. Pass St. John's College on your right and continue past it to the entrance to Wilderness Gate. There is a parking area there and the trail head is clearly marked.

The Dale Ball Trails are a collection of single track trails that wind through the pinon and juniper-covered foothills on the edge of town. There are more than 7 miles of clearly marked and well maintained trails that even young children can navigate. The trails are shared with bikers so keep a look out. To get to the trails follow Upper Canyon Road to the intersection of Cerro Gordo. There is parking at the trail head.

For information on other trails or more information on these, contact one of the outfitters below.

Wild Mountain Outfitters
851 Saint Michael's Drive
(505) 986-1152
www.wildmountainonline.com

Sangre de Cristo Mountain Works
328 South Guadalupe
(505) 984-8221
www.sdcmountainworks.com

Santa Fe Sierra Club
1472 St. Francis Drive
(505) 983-2703
www.riogrande.sierraclub.org/santafe

Tip:
In dry summer months, hiking trails around Santa Fe
will occasionally close because of fire hazard.
It's wise to call first to make sure the trails are open.

Horseback Riding

Are your kids ready to saddle up and play like old west cowboys? There are several outfitters in the area that can make those dreams come true no matter what your skill level. What a great way to see the New Mexico countryside, on the back of a beautiful horse.

Private or small group rides can be arranged, or go along on a group ride and see who you meet along the way. Some of the outfitters can also arrange moonlight rides, rodeos, barbeque and breakfast rides and riding lessons.

Bishop's Lodge Resort
1297 Bishop's Lodge Road
(505) 819-4013
(800) 732-2240
8 And Up (6 for lessons)
www.bishopslodge.com

Broken Saddle Riding Company
Off Highway 14 in the Village of Cerrillos
(505) 424-7774
6 And Up
www.brokensaddle.com

Galarosa Stables
Highway 41 in Galisteo
(505) 466-4653
7 And Up
www.galarosastables.com

Tip:
The Santa Fe Horse Park at the end of Airport Road is a fun place
to spend a weekend afternoon during the summer.
World class polo matches are waged there.
www.horsepark.com

Ice Cream

What is a vacation without a little ice cream? Chocolate, vanilla, strawberry or something a little more exotic—sometimes you just have to have it. When the urge hits you will know where to go.

Haagen Dazs
56 East San Francisco Street
(505) 988-3858

Baskin Robbins
De Vargas Mall
(505) 820-3131

Baskin Robbins
4056 Cerrillos Road
(505) 474-3131

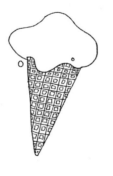
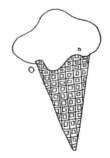

Tip:
The Santa Fe Haagen Dazs is said to sell the most ice cream per capita in the United States.

Jackalope

2820 Cerrillos Road
(505) 471-8539
Monday—Sunday 9 AM-6 PM
www.jackalope.com

No need to travel around the world to do your shopping, simply come to Jackalope. You can find things from China, Vietnam, Mexico, Thailand, Peru, the Southwest and more. Browse through rugs, furniture, clothes, jewelry, housewares, garden equipment, just to name a few of the items you can find here! The indoor/outdoor store, covering several acres, is an explosion of cultures and colors guaranteed to amaze and delight all ages.

There are several areas of specific interest to kids. There is a "Barnyard Animal" area where you can see donkeys, chickens, roosters, goats and other animals depending on the day. The "World Music Stage" has music from around the world. The Aviary houses a variety of birds. For the littlest youngsters, a ride on the hand pushed carousel is sure to be a hit. If all the shopping and walking wear you and the family down, stop by the café for a quick bite or drink.

Tip:
There is so much to see and do here, make sure to budget enough time.

Kasha-Katune Tent Rocks National Monument

Cochiti Pueblo (35 miles south of Santa Fe)
$5 Parking Fee
November through March 8 AM-5 PM
April through October 7 AM-7 PM
Children Over 4 for Climbing

Ever wonder what the surface of the moon looks like? A trip to Kasha-Katune Tent Rocks National Monument may be the closest you will ever come. Here you will find beautiful rock cliffs that have been eroded into indescribable tent shaped formations by wind and water. This is a great place to see some of the areas most stunning geology. There are two hiking trails. The Cave Loop is a 1.2-mile hike that is rated easy and can be undertaken by even the littlest legs with a little help from mom or dad. The longer Slot Canyon hike is a 3-mile round trip hike into a narrow canyon and ending at a mesa top with amazing views of the surrounding mountains. There is not much shade so go early, bring water, snacks and plenty of sunscreen, you will be glad you made the trip.

Driving Tip:
Take I–25 South toward Albuquerque. Take exit 264 (Cochiti Pueblo) and turn right at the stop sign. Travel 8 miles and turn right at the next stop sign. Drive 2.5 miles and turn left at the entrance to Cochiti Pueblo. Turn right onto Peralta Road and travel 4.5 miles on the dirt road to the Ranger Station and parking area.

Lensic Performing Art Center

211 West San Francisco Street
(505) 988-1234
Open Year Round
www.lensic.org

The Lensic was originally a vaudeville house and then was one of Santa Fe's first movie theaters. It is a beautiful art deco theater that was turned into a performing art center in the late 1990s when the multiplexes took over the movie business. On any given evening you can see performances by local, national and international artists. Artists as varied as Savion Glover, the Flying Karamarov Brothers, the Aspen Ballet Company and the Santa Fe Chamber Music Festival have played here. Pick up a schedule at the box office (the theater is two blocks west of the Plaza) or go to their website to see if anything strikes your fancy.

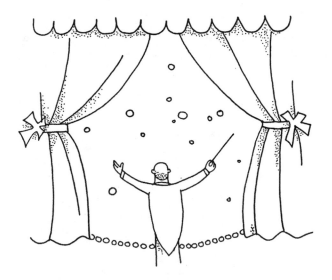

Tip:
Some of the popular events are sold out, but try the box office
the day of the performance for last minute cancellations.

Loretto Chapel

207 Old Santa Fe Trail
(505) 982-0092
Adults $2.50/Children 7–11 $2/Children Under 7 Free
Summer
Monday—Saturday 9AM-6 PM
Sunday 10:30 AM-5 PM
Winter
Monday—Saturday 9 AM-5PM
Sunday 10:30 AM-5 PM
www.lorettochapel.com

This is one of the most popular tourist sites in Santa Fe. Visitors flock here to see the "miraculous staircase", an architectural and engineering wonder. Here's how the story goes: The Sisters of Loretto built the Chapel in the 1870's. The building was fashioned after Sainte-Chapelle in Paris but had one design flaw - there was no way to get to the choir loft. It was becoming more and more difficult for the nuns to climb the high ladders and because of the height of the loft a conventional staircase would take up too much room. So the Sisters said a novena to Saint Joseph the Carpenter. On the last day of their prayers, a mysterious carpenter arrived with only a saw, a carpenter's square, a hammer and tubs to soak wood. Amazingly, he built his staircase with no nails and no visible means of central support. The stairs have 33 steps and two 360-degree turns. The nuns knew they had been blessed with the staircase and tried thanking the mysterious carpenter as legend has it, but they never got the chance. He left as quickly as he arrived without ever asking for payment. You can hear the entire story on audio tape when you visit the chapel. So, sit back in the pews and view this miraculous masterpiece while you listen to the story.

Tip:

This is a tiny chapel. A visit here takes no longer than
twenty minutes, unless you spend a lot of time in the gift shop.

Madrid

22 Miles South of Santa Fe on Highway 14

The first thing you should know is that Madrid is not pronounced like the city in Spain. Instead, sound like a local and call it MAD'-rid. Now, a little about the place. It's an old mining town. In the early 1800s coal was discovered here. The unique geology of the area allowed for the production of hard and soft coal, which had only been found in two other mines in the world. The mining town boomed supplying coal for the Santa Fe Railroad and the government. When coal use declined Madrid became a ghost town. In the 1970s artists moved in and converted the deserted buildings into studios, galleries and shops.

Don't miss the Old Coal Museum, Old West Photography and the Engine House Theater all housed in a building in the center of town. The funky old museum may seem like a glorified junkyard, but remember you are not 8 years old. They have an old steam engine that kids can climb on and even ring the bell. Your kids will have a ball dressing up like cowboys, lawmen, desperados, or Victorian ladies and getting their picture taken at Old West Photography. If you visit on the weekends you may be able to catch a production at the Theater.

Stop at the Mine Shaft Tavern next door for lunch, dinner or a snack and take in the atmosphere of a true roadhouse. It opened in 1946 as the Albuquerque and Cerrillos Coal Company's bar and restaurant. The burgers and chile are great! They serve lunch Monday through Thursday from noon until 3 PM and lunch and dinner Friday through Sunday noon until 8 PM. Red Railyard Collectibles down the street is an authentic Santa Fe Railroad boxcar with fun gifts and souvenirs.

Fun Fact:
If you happen to be in town for the Fourth of July or the Christmas celebration the first two weekends in December you are in for a treat. Catch the parades and festivals that have become a town tradition.

Museum of Indian Art and Culture

710 Camino Lejo
(505) 827-6463
Adults $7/Children Under 16 Free
Tuesday—Sunday 10 AM-5 PM
www.museumofnewmexico.org

Truly a unique stop, the Museum of Indian Art and Culture tells the stories of the people of the Southwest from pre-historic times to the present. The Museum is extremely interactive and kids of all ages will find something to pique their interest.

In the "Here, Now and Always" exhibit an informative video tells of how people came to live in the southwest. After the video you can explore the exhibits describing architecture, art, language, plants, animals, childhood and the land as they relate to Native Americans. There are several interactive features which will intrigue the kids.

The "Southwestern Pottery" exhibit displays pottery from the nineteen pueblos of New Mexico and Arizona. Don't worry, everything is safely behind glass.

You will probably have a difficult time convincing the kids to leave the Discovery Center. They can read books, do art projects, build a house with adobe-like bricks, identify artifacts, practice their weaving skills, do puzzles and play games. Nothing like a little hands on learning.

Tip:
Need refreshment after all this enrichment?
Drop into the Museum Hill Café.
There is a kid's menu and adults can get a quick refreshment.
Sit outside on the patio and enjoy the view of Sun Mountain.

Museum of International Folk Art

706 Camino Lejo
(505) 476-1200
Adults $7/Children Under 16 Free
Tuesday—Sunday 10 AM-5 PM
www.moifa.org

A museum doesn't have to be a children's museum to appeal to the young. The Museum of International Folk Art is a prime example, it is recognized as the home to the world's largest collection of folk art. Among their collections are the 106,000 objects donated by the Girard Family in 1978 and beautifully displayed in the Girard Wing. It is difficult to describe what is in store for the visitor. In each of more than 200 displays you will find intricate scenes of marketplaces, fiestas, festivals, baptisms, bullfights, carnivals, shops, cafes, feast days, villages, ceremonies, processions, dolls, toys and more. The art is representative of countries from around the world including Mexico, Russia, Peru, United States, Mali, Guatemala, India, Indonesia, just to name a few. Children will be endlessly surprised by what is around the next corner.

Explore the museum further and find New Mexican dollhouses, miniature theaters from around the world and ceramic houses of all shapes and sizes. If the little ones get worn out, there is an interactive kid's corner filled with trains, a dollhouse, puppets, Legos, blocks and multicultural books.

Fun Fact:
Step outside and explore Milner Plaza after your museum tour.
You will come across the Plaza Labyrinth. Children will delight in
following the paths and eventually finding themselves in the center.
Make sure they stand directly on the center stone and say a few words.
They will be surprised.

Nambe Falls and Reservoir

Follow 285/84 North out of Santa Fe just past Pojoaque Pueblo.
Turn right onto NM 503 and follow it approximately 3 miles.
Turn right onto Nambe Route 1 to Nambe Falls.

(505) 455-2304
Open Daily 7 AM-6 PM
Site Seeing $5
Fishing $10
Camping $20

Where's the water?!? That is the cry heard from many a tourist and local alike in Santa Fe. When you are hankering for some of the wet stuff head north and spend an afternoon or a day at Nambe Falls and Reservoir. From the Ranger Station you can go to the reservoir for a little swimming, kayaking or fishing. Even more fun is to drive to the camping area and take the easy hike along the river to the falls. It is less than a mile to and from the falls on relatively flat terrain. Most kids three and up should be able to make the trek. Depending on the time of year you may have to walk through the river to get to the falls so don't forget your water shoes or an old pair of sneakers. Take a picnic lunch, lots of water and sunscreen and enjoy the day.

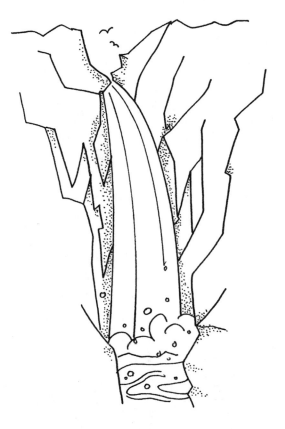

Tip:
This is a perfect opportunity to try Rancho de Chimayo for lunch
or dinner. It's a beautiful drive from the falls to Chimayo.
Read the review on page 107 to see if it's right for the family,
it really is an experience not to be missed.

The Oldest House in the USA

215 East De Vargas Street
(505) 988-4127
Adults $1
Monday—Saturday
Winter: 10 AM-3 PM
Summer: 9 AM-5 PM

Legend holds that this is the oldest house in the United States. Although there is no specific proof of its age, the house is part of Santa Fe's folklore. It is believed that the house is built on the foundation of an Indian Pueblo dating from 1200 AD. In the 1600s Spanish settlers looking for a permanent settlement found the area around the house, known as El Barrio de Analco, to be the perfect location. It was on high ground near the river north of the neighborhood. The two room house depicts life as it may have been for the early settlers. The vigas, or beams, in the ceiling date from 1646. Local folklore tells of witches and ghosts associated with the house. One such story can be read in the second room of the house—sure to be of interest to the kids.

Tip:

Make a side trip to the San Miguel Mission Church across the street. It was most likely built in the early 1600s by the Tlascalan Indians from Mexico, who had settled in Santa Fe when the city was founded in 1610. Beneath the altar you can see stone and dirt flooring that is thought to be from a chapel that was built by Pueblo Indians who occupied the area until the 1300s.

The Painted Dish

839 Paseo de Peralta, Suites E and F
(505) 995-1165
Monday—Saturday 10 AM-5 PM
Sunday Noon-5 PM

On a beautiful day in Santa Fe, there are plenty of things to do with your children. When it is a cold or wet day you are a bit more challenged. That's when a place like The Painted Dish really comes in handy. Open seven days a week, this is a hands-on studio where children pick out a piece of pottery, select the colors of paint they want to use and go to work. There are a variety of items at a variety of prices——everything from large serving platters to decorative little boxes. You can end up spending a lot of money here, so you may want to give your kids a limit. The coffee mugs are a great choice, you will probably use them every morning.

Tip:

In the summer, the Painted Dish holds a kids summer pottery camp.
You drop your kids off for two hours, let them choose something
to paint and enjoy some time for yourself. The women who work at
the Painted Dish are helpful and patient with the children.
Call to find out if any special events are planned.
This is a fun activity for children and for creative parents as well.

Palace of the Governors

105 West Palace Avenue
(505) 827-6463
Adults $7/Children Under 16 Free
Tuesday—Saturday 10 AM-5 PM
www.palaceofthegovernors.org

According to the plaque at the entrance to the Palace of the Governors the building was originally El Palacio Real, a fortress and castle built by the Spanish in 1610-1612. It was the seat of government under the flags of the Spanish, the Mexicans and the Americans. From 1610 through 1910 it was the residence of over one hundred Governors and Captains and is the oldest public building in the United States.

This is a great place for your kids to trace the history of New Mexico over the past 400 years. The museum houses exhibits from the Spanish Colonial times, the Mexican occupation, the conflict between the Mexicans and the Territorialists, the Territorial Period, and the period of statehood.

The first New Mexico flag is on display as is a New Mexico flag that was taken to the moon on Apollo 11. Rifles, pistols, revolvers, swords, historic instruments, a horse drawn hearse, a 1900s surrey, and much more are all on display. Kids can also learn about the history of the Santa Fe Trail.

Be sure to ask at the front desk for special workbooks for kids. They often have very detailed activity books relating to current exhibits for kids to have and use during their visit.

Tip:
Under the portal outside of the Palace
is the Native American Artisans Program.
Here Native Americans from all nineteen New Mexico Pueblos
display and sell their wares. You will see metalwork, pottery,
jewelry, sand painting, and other goods for sale.
It is like no other marketplace in the world!

The Plaza

San Francisco Street, Washington Street, Palace Avenue, Lincoln Avenue

Young or old you have to start at the beginning and in Santa Fe that would be the Plaza—the center of everything; art, culture, history, shopping, food. You and the kids can find almost anything you want here. The Plaza was established in 1610 and was originally used to graze livestock and to hold town meetings. Buildings started cropping up in the 1700s and 1800s and as the town grew shade trees, benches and monuments were added.

The southeast corner of the Plaza was the end of the historic Santa Fe Trail and the building on that site was a confectionery, how happy that must have made children after a long journey west! Your kids can have a sweet treat after their own journey, Senor Murphy Candymaker, a Santa Fe institution, is located in the base of the La Fonda Hotel (100 East San Francisco Street).

Browsing the shops and galleries on and around the Plaza can be fun for all ages. Check out Yippee Yi Yo Gifts (54 East San Francisco Street), the Five and Dime General Store (58 East San Fracisco Street), Dressman's Gifts (58 Lincoln Street) and Doodlets Shop (120 Don Gaspar Avenue) just to name a few. Your kids will have a ball browsing through everything these shops have to offer. While you are in the Five and Dime, try one of their famous Frito Pies, the best in town. They actually serve it in a Frito bag. If the chile is too hot, their hot dogs aren't bad either. Grab a scoop of Haagen Dasz ice cream from next door (56 East San Francisco Street) and head over to one of the benches in the center of the Plaza. If you're lucky there may be some entertainment at the Pavilion on the Palace Avenue side of the Plaza.

Tip:
Almost every weekend in the summer there is an art show or festival on the Plaza. July is Spanish Market, August is Indian Market, September is Fiesta and there are arts and crafts fairs in between.

Quiet Time

Santa Fe Public Library

There are three public libraries in Santa Fe. They each offer a wide variety of children's activities and events.

Main Library
145 Washington Avenue
(505) 955-6781
Monday—Thursday 10 AM-9 PM
Friday—Saturday 10 AM-6 PM
Sunday 1 PM-5PM
www.santafelibrary.org

Oliver La Farge Branch Library
1730 Llano Street
(505) 955-4870

Bookstop at Villa Linda Mall
4250 Cerrillos Road
(505) 955-2980

The Main Library is the type of old-fashioned library most of us fondly remember from our own childhood years. It's filled with wooden tables and has all kinds of nooks and crannies. The children's area is tucked away upstairs and is a great place to spend a quiet hour or two reading books or playing educational games on the computers. There's a terrific reading program in the summer, complete with puppeteers, magicians, storytelling and other activities. Call for a complete list of special event information.

Fun Fact:

If you don't have a local library card, but want to take something home
here's a suggestion: Print out coloring pages from the PBS website on
one of the upstairs computers. We like Sagwa, Dragon Tales and Clifford.
If you aren't sure how to work the computers, the aide will help you.

Rafting

Looking for a little white water adventure? The Rio Grande and Rio Chama boast some great runs for kids and adults. Half-day, full-day and overnight trips can be arranged and you are sure to see some beautiful scenery.

Kokopelli Rafting Adventures
(505) 983-3734
www.kokopelliraft.com

Far Flung Adventures
(800) 359-2627
www.farflung.com

Santa Fe Rafting Company
(505) 988-4914
www.santaferafting.com

Tip:
Each outfitter has its own age limit for each run. Make sure to ask about your youngsters and find out if they can come along for the ride.

Salvador Perez Park

601 Alta Vista Street
(505) 955-2604

Locals call this the Train Park. When you arrive at this conveniently located park off Saint Francis Drive, you'll know why. There's a real locomotive surrounded by a fence in the middle of the park. There are several different play areas in the park. One playground is ideal for those under the age of about six. Lots of jungle gyms, swings and slides. In another area of the park, there's a second play area better suited for older kids. It has high monkey bars and more difficult climbing equipment. There is a soccer field in good condition, but the tennis courts are rundown with lots of cracks in them. This is a good park for dog lovers with plenty of open space for your canine to stretch his legs. Just be sure to clean up after him if he makes a mess (bring your own pooper scooper). There are also covered picnic tables to get you out of the sun for lunch or a snack.

Tip:
Across the street, there's a nice, newly renovated indoor pool. Admission to the pool is by session so make sure you call ahead to get the current schedule. There are also weights, treadmills, stairmasters, yoga classes and other activities available at the facility.

Recreation Center
Monday—Friday 6 AM-8:30 PM
Saturday 10 AM-7 PM
Sunday 10 AM-6:30 PM
Children $0.75/Adults $1.85

Santa Fe Children's Museum

1050 Old Pecos Trail
(505) 989-8359
$4 per person
$1 for New Mexico residents on Sunday
Wednesday—Sunday 10 AM-5 PM
www.santafechildrensmuseum.org

The Children's Museum is a treasure for kids of all ages. It will keep kids happily occupied for hours. The theme here is hands-on and there are plenty of volunteers to assist. They're big on interactive stuff and the kids love it. For the younger ones, the face-painting station may be the first stop - a mirrored vanity stocked with every shade imaginable of do-it-yourself face-painting crayons. The children also seem to swarm to the bubble-making station where they use a giant wand to create life-sized bubbles from soapy water. There's also a cozy arts and crafts room. The kids put on aprons and cut, glue, draw and create their own masterpieces. Special art projects with local artists are ongoing- you could be making yarn art, pottery, sand art or nature art just to name a few. For bigger children (weighing at least 50 pounds) the rock-climbing wall is a blast. Volunteers strap them in and help them negotiate the vertical climb.

And there's more- a reading nook, a dress-up area, water play, and a jungle gym where toddlers can climb and explore. But don't leave the Museum yet, the outdoor grounds are beautiful. There are areas to dig in the sand, climb a tree house, bang drums, ring chimes or simply sit and enjoy the scenery. Animal lovers will enjoy the museum's menagerie of animals. There are rabbits, rats, snakes, exotic birds and even a huge tray filled with earthworms. Don't forget to visit the greenhouse where most of the creatures are kept. There's also a good arts and crafts table in the greenhouse.

Sound like a lot to do? There is. That's why the Santa Fe Children's Museum is a favorite with locals and visitors alike. It should be one of your first stops in the City Different. Your kids will thank you and will probably beg to come back.

Fun Fact:
Once a month, on a Friday night, the museum hosts a special event called Kids' Night. Parents drop their kids off at the museum at 5:30 and pick them up at 9:30. The children eat pizza, make arts and crafts projects and have the run of the museum. Such fun doesn't come cheap. $40 for one child. $30 for additional kids. Reservations are necessary.

Santa Fe Climbing Center

825 Early Street Suite A
(505) 986-8944
Day Pass $12/Children Under 11 $8
Rental Package $5
www.climbsantafe.com

Looking for a way to let your children burn some energy? This climbing gym may be just the thing. On Saturday afternoons from 1:00-3:00 or on Monday evenings from 5:00-7:00 you can bring the kids here, help get them strapped into safety ropes and watch them try to master a very tall climbing wall. This is best for children five years old and older.

Volunteer belayers are available during these sessions to help kids negotiate the wall. Call for prices and to make reservations for special outings.

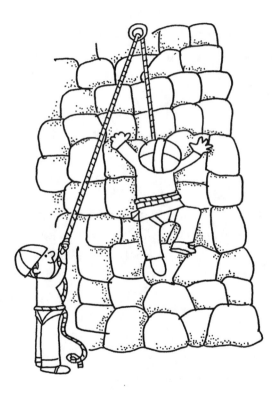

Tip:

The center also offers outdoor rock climbing and mountain hiking.

Santa Fe Ski Basin/Hyde State Park

Highway 475 (Artist Road) 15 miles northeast of Santa Fe
(505) 982-4429
www.skisantafe.com

Santa Fe is a great place to take children skiing. For starters, it's a short, hassle-free drive from the historic downtown area. On most days, it will take you less than 45 minutes. Once you arrive, you'll be surrounded by the beautiful Sangre de Cristo mountains where all levels of skiers can enjoy world-class skiing on a 12,175 foot mountain. There are 44 trails to choose from…the majority of them are intermediate or beginner slopes that are family friendly. For the experts, there are plenty of black diamonds, too.

If your children have never skied before, or if they simply need to brush up on their skills they'll definitely want to check out Chipmunk Corner. This is a full-service, on-site children's complex complete with ski and snow play areas and a rope tow. For children four and older there are half-days and full-days of ski school ($64 for a full day, $48 for a half day). Here's how it works: you check in as soon as the center opens and fill out the necessary paperwork. Then, the instructors divide the young skiers into small classes according to their ability.

After a couple of hours in the snow, the kids head inside where lunch is provided. For those staying all day, there are more lessons in the afternoon. For toddlers and children too young to ski, sign them up for Snowplay, a great introduction to the skiing environment. Weather permitting (and it usually does) the children head outside where they play on sleds and slosh around in the snow. Then, they come inside and climb on a little jungle gym, play with books and toys, do arts and crafts and eat lunch. A nursery service is provided for ages 3 months to 3 years ($12 per hour). Space is limited, so reservations are required.

Call Ski Santa Fe at (505) 988-9636. The ski season generally runs from Thanksgiving until Easter…depending on the amount of snow.

Fun Fact:
During September and early October the Aspen trees around the Ski Basin are stunning. People flock up the mountain to view the brilliant yellow, orange and red trees. You can pull over to the side of the road at various places or go all the way up the mountain. Once there, ride the ski lift for the most amazing views. The lift costs $7 roundtrip. Children under 46 inches tall are free.

Tip:
The food is very good at the Ski Basin. We love the grilled chile cheeseburgers. Some people who don't even ski told us they come here specifically for the burgers.

Santa Fe Southern Railway

410 South Guadalupe Street
(505) 989-8600
(888) 989-8600
Prices Vary
Year Round
www.sfsr.com

Take a train ride through Northern New Mexico's beautiful high desert. You will ride on early-century coaches, an open observation flat car and mid-century luxury lounge cars. You can chose from a lunch or barbeque run to Lamy or a shorter ride to the Galisteo Basin. Special sunset trips are available in the summer as well. Your kids will feel like they have gone back in time.

A favorite trip for kids is the barbeque train to Lamy. Board the train in the late afternoon at the historic station on Guadalupe Street. You may want to stop in the gift shop first for some memorabilia, information about the trains or some fun activities for the kids. On board there is a snack bar and an adult bar for libations. However, supplies are limited so you may want to bring your own. The train will travel south through Santa Fe into the open desert and on to Lamy. Kids love standing on the open observation car and waving at passersby. The conductor gives out pinwheels that are a blast in the wind. When you arrive at Lamy a fantastic barbeque is set up under a big Cottonwood tree. A western musician serenades you while you enjoy your meal.

Back on board for the trip back to Santa Fe your kids will marvel at the thousands of stars they can see in a New Mexico sky. You will arrive at the station with a happy, well fed and tired gang.

Fun Fact.
This isn't just a trip for tourists.
The vintage train still transports freight.

Shidoni Foundry

1508 Bishop's Lodge Road
(5 miles north of Paseo de Peralta)
(505) 988-8001
Free
Bronze Gallery: Monday—Saturday 9 AM-3 PM
Gardens: Daylight Hours
Foundry: Monday—Friday Noon-1 PM, Saturday 9 AM-5 PM
Bronze Pours: Saturday Afternoons
www.Shidoni.com

The Shidoni Foundry is just a short drive from downtown Santa Fe and is well worth the quick trip. Pack a few snacks, load up the family and head five miles north on Bishop's Lodge Road to the scenic town of Tesuque. Once there, turn left into Shidoni, where you'll find lush sculpture gardens, a bronze art foundry and a gallery of fabulous bronze sculptures. It's all located on an eight-acre apple orchard, which makes for a beautiful setting.

Young children will enjoy running through the green, manicured grounds and looking at the hundreds of interesting pieces of art. Take a break on the many benches and picnic tables scattered throughout the grounds. Talk about a perfect place for a picnic.

Young and old alike will be fascinated when they see the main attraction. Every Saturday afternoon, there are several bronze pourings. It's quite dramatic watching the workers in heat-proof suits pouring 2000-degree molten metal into ceramic shell molds. Sure, it's a great tourist attraction, but what the foundry does even better is to provide a great resource for sculptors and artists. It seems to do all of these things extremely well.

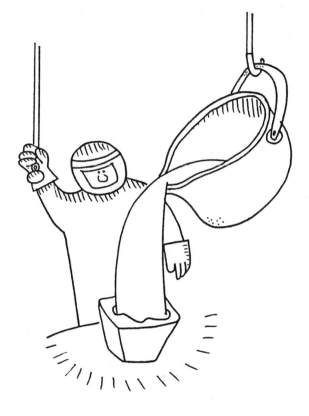

Fun Fact:
If you have a few thousand extra dollars to spare,
you can buy a one-of-a-kind bronze sculpture from one of
100 different sculptors from all over the country.

Sledding

When it starts snowing in Santa Fe, the kids can't wait to go outside and play. A favorite thing for locals to do is grab a sled and head for a hill. Sledding is extremely popular in these parts because it's so darn easy and cheap (except for the few dollars you spend buying a plastic sled). Plus, you don't have to drive very far to find a perfect spot. A great stop for young children is the Msgr. Patrick Smith park on East Alameda near Gonzales Street. There are gentle hills that are perfect (not too scary) for kids about eight years old and younger. Want to do some serious sledding? Head toward the Santa Fe Ski Basin About eight miles from town you'll see Cottam's Ski Shop on the right hand. Directly behind the shop is a great place for sledding. Locals flock here when the conditions are right. One run is perfect for all ages. Park your car, trek up the hill, hop on your sled and cruise on down. Whee!

Younger children may want to ride with a parent, older sibling or friend. There's also a fast run for more daring sledders. Teenagers seem to love shooting down on inner tubes. Best of all, it's free. Just be sure to wear warm gloves, snow pants and snow shoes. It gets wet and cold.

Fun Fact:
You can buy inexpensive sleds all over town.
We bought ours at Target for less than $10.00. Walmart and Big 5 Sports
(all located on Cerrillos Road) are also good bets.

Sp nish coloni l Art us um

750 Camino Lejo
(505) 982-2226
$6 out-of-state/$3 in-state residents
Tuesday thru Sunday 10 AM-5 PM
www.spanishcolonial.org

Founded by the Spanish Colonial Arts Society, this museum houses 3,000 objects from its collection. New Mexico was once the northernmost point of the Spanish empire and this collection represents the rich cultural and arts tradition still evident in the area.

The museum is small enough not to overwhelm kids. It is housed in a home designed by John Gaw Meem, an architect that had a major impact on the development of New Mexico's Spanish Colonial/Pueblo revival building style. Here you will see tools, jewelry, a room set up as it may have looked in the 1800s, and a remarkable collection of bultos (wood carved saints) and retablos. There is a children's room in one of the back rooms of the museum where kids can dress in period clothes, do art projects and puzzles and read books. There is also an area where Spanish Colonial Art made by children is displayed.

Fun Fact:
Make sure your kids get the "scavenger hunt" handout at the front desk. It will take them through the museum looking for specific items. It is amazing how much they can learn without even trying.

Tinkertown Museum

121 Sandia Crest Road (35 miles south of Santa Fe)
Sandia Park
(505) 281-5233
Adults $3/Children 4–16 $1
April through October 9 AM-6 PM
www.tinkertown.com

It is diffucult to describe Tinkertown, you really have to see it to belive it. Ross Ward, a painter, carver and collector turned his collection of Americana into what he calls a "folk art environment." The miniature wood carved figures range from cowboys in a western town to circus performers under the big-top to weddings in early America. For twenty-five cents you can have your fortune told by an animatronic psychic. Another machine will examine and determine your physique. The 22 room museum is surrounded by walls formed by more than 50,000 glass bottles. Wagon wheels, old-fashioned store fronts and western memorabilia make the exterior as interesting as the interior. It will take you many, many trips to see everything that the museum holds. Don't forget a quick stop in the gift shop.

Tip:

This is a great extension to a trip to Madrid. It's an easy and beautiful 20 minute drive south from Madrid (see page 54).

Useful Publications

Several publications can give you great information about what is going on in Santa Fe at any given time. Tumbleweeds and New Mexico Kids (www.newmexico-kids.com) are publications geared specifically towards kids. They have listings for everything from classes to childcare and plays to pottery. You can pick them up at many places around town but you are sure to find them at the Santa Fe Children's Museum, the Video Library and the Santa Fe Public Library. Tumbleweeds is published quarterly and New Mexico Kids is published bi-monthly.

Two weekly publications can also offer you a wealth of information. They are not specific to kids but they do have sections for kids and you are sure to discover something of interest to your family. The Santa Fe Reporter (www.sfreporter.com) is free and comes out on Wednesdays. It can be found anywhere newspapers are sold. In the Friday edition of the New Mexican you will find Pasatiempo (www.epasatiempo.com), which also spells out everything that is going on in the week and weeks ahead.

Video Library

120 East Marcy Street
(505) 983-3321

For that rainy afternoon when mom and dad just want to rest or for the evening out when you're not doing Santa Fe with Kids, head to the Video Library. This is not your typical video store. Sure they have all of the new releases on video and DVD but that is just the tip of the iceberg. It feels like they have everything ever made and if they don't they will find it for you. The owner of the store is a wealth of information. Just give her the age range of your kids, a few of their interests and poof! you have the perfect movie for your family. What could be better? Plus, there is free parking here, a rarity in Santa Fe.

Tip:
Every day there is a different "special offer" at the Video Library. For instance on Wednesday kids movies are fifty cents. Check it out.

Wheelwright Museum

704 Camino Lejo
(505) 982-4636 or (800) 607-4636
Free
Monday—Saturday 10 AM-5 PM
Sunday 1 PM-5 PM
Closed Mondays
www.wheelwright.org

The Wheelwright Museum is a lovely small museum that sits on Santa Fe's Museum Hill. Walk inside and see all types of Native American art... from 300-year old clay pots to traditional Indian clothing. For children, there is a small desk where they can draw pictures and write in a museum journal. Downstairs, the kids will enjoy The Case Trading Post Museum Shop. Designed to resemble an early Navajo trading post, it's one of America's most famous museum shops. Browse through hundreds of items such as jewelry, rugs, pottery, baskets and books. This museum is probably best suited for older children who have an interest in Native American art and history. The little ones will like the large teepee in front of the museum. Also, on the second Saturday of every month the Wheelwright holds a children's story hour and related art projects. Call for details.

Fun Fact:

On Saturday and Sunday evenings in July and August, famous storyteller
Joe Hayes entertains families on the museum's patio.
Sit back, enjoy the beautiful mountains and hear tall tales and legends
of New Mexico and the Southwest. His stories are not to be missed.
Bring a blanket and jacket, it gets chilly.

Wood Gormley Playground

Booth Street Between Don Gaspar and Weber Street

Across the street from Wood Gormley Elementary School is a block long playground, which is a great stop for children of all ages. The play area closest to Don Gaspar consists of four interconnected climbing structures suitable for kids three and up (the sign says 5 to 12 but 3 year olds will be thrilled). Four swings and updated monkey bars round out this first area. Beyond a large grassy field (rare for Santa Fe) is a second play area with a larger climbing structure and six more swings for the older kids. A small basketball court with four hoops is adjacent to this area. Beyond the court are two nine-foot climbing walls, six chin up bars, balance beams and parallel bars. There are picnic tables and benches for parents to watch their children having hours of fun.

Tip:
There are no facilities at the playground. Make sure you stock up on water and snacks and make a pit stop before you come.
Also, the playground is not open to the public
while school is in session.

X-tras

It's miserable being sick when you're on vacation. We hope it doesn't happen during your Santa Fe visit, but if it does here's some useful information.

Medical Care

Urgent Care Santa Fe
2801 Rodeo Road
(505) 474-0120
10 AM-10 PM

This walk-in clinic is the place to go if you have a minor injury or illness. During regular business hours, there are several physicians available. At night or on weekends, you might see a nurse practitioner. This clinic sees patients more quickly and is cheaper than the emergency room.

Saint Vincent Hospital
455 St. Michael's Drive
(505) 983-3361 main number
(505) 995-3934 emergency
www.stvin.org

This is Santa Fe's only full-service hospital. It is where you must go if you have a serious problem or require an ambulance.

24-hour Pharmacies

Walgreens Drug Stores
1096 South Saint Francis Drive
(505) 982-4643
And
3298 Cerrillos Road
(505) 474-3532

Both Walgreens locations can fill a prescription anytime of the night or day. You can also pick up those essentials you forgot to pack.

YoYos, Etc.

Eventually you are going to need some supplies. Whether it's a toy to keep the kiddies busy in the hotel room, an activity book for the car, a pair of new shoes for hiking or a bathing suit that you forgot to pack the stores listed below should cover your needs in any emergency.

Toyopolis
66 West Marcy
(505) 988-8994

Merry Go Round
150 Washington Avenue
(505) 988-5422

Gap Kids
Villa Linda Mall
(505) 471-2326

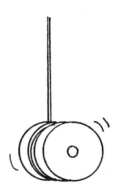

The Mall

Going to a mall probably isn't the first thing you'll rush to do in Santa Fe. However, if you need a big department store (Dillards, Mervyns or Sears) this is the place. You'll find the usual mall stores, including a Victoria's Secret, Gap and Gap Kids. There are also two movie-multiplexes, a library and a carousel that young children love.

Villa Linda Mall
4250 Cerrillos Road (corner of Rodeo Road)
(505) 473-4253
www.villalindamall.com

The Grocery Store

Need a grocery store? There are many small, specialty markets. However, this is the place to go if you need to stock up.

Albertsons Food and Drug
3001 South Saint Francis Drive
in the De Vargas Shopping Center

Zozobra

Fort Marcy Park
The First Thursday after Labor Day
2pm to dusk
$10 at gate, $5 at Whole Foods and local banks
Kids under Six Free
www.zozobra.com

Ready to kiss your gloom and doom goodbye? The burning of Zozobra is the way Santa Feans see their worries go up in flames each year. In case you're wondering, Zozobra is a 50-foot marionette decorated as Old Man Gloom. He's rather frightening looking with a white face and hollow eyes. He symbolizes all the bad that happened in the previous year and that's why he is set ablaze in front of tens of thousands of people at Fort Marcy Park on the Thursday night after Labor Day. It's a fabulous, extravagant event that's been going on for more than 80 years as a way to kick off the city's Fiesta.

At Zozobra, you'll find food, dancing, entertainment and amazing fireworks. And finally, the big finale is the burning of Zozobra on the park's baseball field shortly after dark. People of all ages come to the park early in the day with their lawn chairs and picnic blankets and stay until after the burning. However, be warned, this all can be frightening to young children. The crowd really gets into the act by yelling "burn him, burn him" and moaning and groaning. Also, there are so many people crammed into the park that you must keep a close eye on junior so he doesn't get lost. However, for older kids or mature younger ones, this is a one-of a kind event. In fact, everyone needs to see Zozobra at least once. It's Santa Fe's version of Mardi Gras…and it all happens in one flamboyant night.

If you can't stand the crowd, stay at home and watch the festivities on the public access television station. Or try to finagle an invitation to someone's rooftop for a great view of the action. Many local businesses close early on the day of Zozobra so their employees can enjoy the festivities. This is the city's biggest and wildest annual celebration.

Tip:
Take a park n ride shuttle bus to Zozobra from one of many locations around town. Parking can be a real headache on this day.

Restaurants

Santa Fe is a city of food. It is known for its world-class restaurants and its distinctive cuisine. Just because you have your kids along doesn't mean you can't enjoy all that Santa Fe has to offer. We have listed several restaurants that make it very easy for a family to enjoy great food and drink while keeping the kiddies busy and not annoying people at the neighboring table.

Blue Corn Café

This place may be listed in the dictionary under kid-friendly. Located just off the Plaza, the open and bright second floor space is bustling and happily loud with contented kids and grownups. The extensive kids menu doubles as a coloring sheet, with crayons on the side. Kiddie drinks come in colorful plastic cups with spill proof tops. For the parents there are New Mexican specialties, salads, burgers and sandwiches. They also have 23 types of tequilas, 13 different margaritas and six ales from their own microbrewery. Thirsty anyone?

Lunch and Dinner
Open 7 Days
133 West Water Street
(505) 984-1800

NOTE: There is a second café located across from Villa Linda Mall. It is bigger than the downtown location and would make a great stop if you are on the south side of town.

Lunch and Dinner
Open 7 Days
4056 Cerrillos Road
(505) 438-1800

Bobcat Bite

If you are a burger lover this place is not to be missed. They serve the best green chile cheeseburgers around, as well as pork chops, steaks, and chicken. But the majority of their business has to be the burgers that made them famous. There are photos of bobcats on the walls and a story of the place on the menu—both of which will intrigue the kids. The small roadhouse only has a few tables and bar seats and it is only open four days a week. Make sure you go early for lunch or dinner or you will be waiting a while for a seat.

Lunch and Dinner
Wednesday—Saturday
442 Old Las Vegas Highway
(505) 983-5319

Bumblebee's Baja Grill

There is a buzz about Bumblebee's and you won't be disappointed! Fast, fresh and way above-average Mexican fast food. The kids' menu includes a huge serving of cheese quesadillas or tacos, rice and beans, lemonade and a lollipop. For grown-ups the mahi-mahi salad is delicious as are the other fresh and satisfying New Mexican dishes. Sitting on the patio is especially enjoyable. Bring your own crayons and coloring books. No table service. Perfect for a cheap, easy, quick meal.

Lunch and Dinner
Open 7 Days
301 Jefferson Street
(505) 820-2862

Celebrations

A fantastic respite from the gallery hoping and strolling on Canyon Road, this funky restaurant is a favorite of locals and visitors alike. There is a great patio out front where you can people watch to your hearts content. The menu is eclectic and everyone is sure to find something to tickle their fancy. They don't have a separate kids menu, but they have great eggs, burgers, sandwiches and salads. When your kids need to use the facilities make sure you warn them about the carved cowboy on the bench in the bathroom or you are sure to hear a scream!

Breakfast and Lunch
Open 7 Days
613 Canyon Road
(505) 989-8904

Cowgirl Hall of Fame

Of all the Santa Fe restaurants, this is our family favorite for lunch and dinner. It's a great place to sit outside with the kids.. either on the front patio where there's often live music... or in the back with picnic tables and a playground. The kids menu serves up corn dogs, mac n' cheese, burgers,ribs and more. The kids love the Cowkid cocktail (a fruity, Sprite concoction in a frosty mug). Another plus: a fun cowgirl coloring page with crayons. Reservations are suggested.... especially if you want to sit on the small, back patio.

Lunch and Dinner
Open 7 Days
Breakfast Saturday and Sunday
319 S. Guadalupe Street
(505) 982-2565

Guadalupe Café

Sunday Brunch and breakfast are legendary at the Guadalupe Café and they have a great kid's menu. It includes pancakes, eggs, breakfast burritos and French toast- all reasonably priced. The pancakes are definitely not child-sized. Instead, they are huge and fluffy with maple syrup on the side. Honestly, two or three young children could easily share one order. The adult menu is delicious, too. Try the chorizo omelet. Come armed with crayons and paper and other stuff. The service can be a bit slow but this place is worth a trip.

Breakfast, Lunch and Dinner
Tuesday—Sunday
422 Old Santa Fe Trail
(505) 982-9762

Harry's Roadhouse

It doesn't get much better than this on a warm summer evening. Arrive early (before 6:00) and you'll probably get to sit on the beautiful back patio. Inside is okay, too. Kids immediately get an intricate sheet of artwork and a set of crayons. They're occupied and you're happy. The kids menu is great (chicken strips, burgers and other home style cooking). Margaritas for mom and dad are among the best in town. Reservations are accepted for parties of six or more. Arrive too late and you'll have a long wait. Time it right and you'll be glad you came.

Breakfast, Lunch and Dinner
Open 7 Days
96B Old Las Vegas Highway
(505) 989-4629

Il Vicino

We conducted a very unscientific poll of local nine and ten year olds and they told us this is one of their favorite restaurants. In fact, they think the pizza here is the best in town. We also like it. It's extremely convenient if you're staying downtown and want to walk to a restaurant. It's located next to the El Dorado Hotel and down the street from the Lensic Theatre. If you're driving, you can park in the back. Order at the counter, take a seat and waiters serve you. As for the food, there's not a specific kids menu. However, there is a tasty 6" pizza for less than $4.00. The pizza is thin and crispy and cooked to perfection. There are also salads and pasta dishes. The spinach salad with pine nuts is divine.

Lunch and Dinner
Open 7 Days
321 W. San Francisco Street
(505) 986-8700

La Choza Restaurant

This is the sister restaurant to the Shed. Just like the Shed the setting is funky and the food is fabulous. The menus are similar but there are a few departures. More locals probably frequent this spot because it is away from the hustle and bustle of downtown and there is ample parking. There are several choices for kids but not a separate kids menu. Bring your own toys to keep the little ones occupied and ask for a table outside. You may hear the Santa Fe Southern Railroad passing by during your meal. Hold on to your plates.

Lunch and Dinner
Monday—Saturday
905 Alarid Street
(505) 982-0909

Maria's New Mexican Kitchen

This busy, bustling restaurant is a great choice if you're craving a big plate of New Mexican food. Locals and tourists flock here for the festive atmosphere and good food. Choose from at least a dozen appetizers (the guacamole and nachos are hard to beat) or from the extensive menu. For younger ones, how about a child's plate with either a taco or burrito? Other items kids may enjoy are cheeseburgers, fajitas, ribs, enchiladas, quesadillas, sopapillas... the list goes on. Bring coloring books and crayons for entertainment. As for adults, there are more than 100 margaritas on the menu. They're fresh and good. Make reservations. Maria's is always busy.

Lunch and Dinner
Open 7 Days
555 West Cordova Road
(505) 983-7929

The Pantry

You must arrive early in the morning at this popular local restaurant. The place gets crowded with everyone from construction workers to skiers to families with young children. After a visit here, you'll know why. Day in and day out, the folks here serve up fresh, good, affordable New Mexican food. Breakfasts are especially good. For less than $3.00 your little one can have pancakes, French toast or an egg with bacon or sausage. Or for a buck more, order a blueberry or strawberry stuffed pancake. Yum. There's also a good lunch and dinner menu for kids. Plus, they have a very hip, interesting coloring page. Parents will love this down-to-earth diner, too. We suggest anything with a hearty dose of green chile.

Breakfast, Lunch and Dinner
Open 7 Days
1820 Cerrillos Road
(505) 986-0022

The Pink Adobe

Ok, so maybe it's not what jumps to mind when you want a meal with kids, but The Pink Adobe is a Santa Fe tradition and a trip to town would not be complete without a visit here. The décor is fun for the kids especially if you sit in the tail of the dragon (an area behind the famous Dragon Room bar). There is a kid's menu and the little ones may just find something on the regular menu—the restaurant serves continental cuisine. Go early and enjoy—you'll be glad you did.

Lunch Monday—Friday
Dinner Open 7 Days
406 Old Santa Fe Trail
(505) 983-7712

The Plaza Restaurant

This may look like your typical diner, but don't be fooled. The similarities stop with the décor and the menu that runs from Grilled Trout to Gyros. The food is fabulous and everyone will find something on the menu to satisfy their appetite. Breakfast runs the gamut from pancakes to Huevos Rancheros. The blueberry muffins are legendary. Lunch and dinner menus include salads, sandwiches, American specialties and of course the ever present New Mexican dishes. The chile is HOT and fantastic! There is a great kids menu although if yours have big appetites they can find something on the regular menu as well. The kiddie drinks come in spill proof cups, which makes everyone's meal more peaceful. They don't have crayons and coloring pages but there is a box of emergency Legos at the hostess station.

Breakfast, Lunch and Dinner
Open 7 Days
On the Plaza
54 Lincoln Avenue
(505) 982-1664

Rancho de Chimayo

This is a great spot to include in one of your day trips outside of Santa Fe or as a destination all its own. Housed in a century old adobe home and surrounded by three mountain ranges, the restaurant serves excellent native New Mexican specialties. It is truly a beautiful location. There is a kid's menu and a family atmosphere so no need to worry if junior is not in peak form. Try to get a table on the patio and enjoy the beautiful surroundings and great food, it is definitely worth the trip!

Lunch and Dinner Open 7 Days May-October
Closed Mondays November—April
Breakfast Saturday and Sunday
County Road 98
Chimayo
(505) 984-2100

Santa Fe Bar & Grill

Some people wouldn't consider going to a restaurant in a mall and if you're that type, you should reconsider. Santa Fe Bar & Grill is located in the DeVargas Center...an older mall close to downtown. If you want something simple and hassle-free give the Bar & Grill a try. The patio is very comfortable and always filled with locals. The hostess will provide you with coloring books and crayons to keep the kids happy. The children's menu is surprisingly good and seems healthier than many places. It includes grilled chicken tenders, pasta with tomato sauce (very good) and a cheeseburger. For parents, the soups, salads, sandwiches and burgers (even Atkins' style) are great. This is a casual, contemporary bistro where children are welcome.

Lunch and Dinner
Open 7 Days
DeVargas Center
Paseo de Peralta and Guadalupe Street
(505) 982-3033

The Shed

The Shed is a Santa Fe institution. Right off the Plaza, it's also convenient. The food is excellent. Kids love the charro beans and tortillas. Other kids' items include quesadillas, burritos and tacos. For parents wanting a good New Mexican meal with delicious chile, the Shed is a great choice. Most people would agree that the red chile here is the best in town. Plan to eat early with little kids. The tables are close together and it gets crowded. Coloring pages and crayons are provided so settle in and try to get a seat on the patio.

Lunch and Dinner
Monday—Saturday
113 ½ E. Palace Avenue
(505) 982-9030

Tia Sophia's

Looking for a great place near downtown for breakfast? This may be the spot. For adults, the huevos rancheros, omelettes and breakfast burritos are delicious. For kids, how about a mini-breakfast of eggs, bacon and toast for $2.25? The menu also offers a $1.50 PB&J, cereal or a tortilla with melted cheese. Yum. Lunch is fine, too. There's a taco plate, cheeseburger and bean burrito on the children's menu. The only downfall? You may have to wait for a table. This place is popular, especially for breakfast. Bring crayons and paper for the kids. Be careful if you're not accustomed to New Mexican chile. The menu says "not responsible for too hot chile". Check out the bookshelf at the front of the restaurant. It's stocked with dozens of children's classics.

Breakfast and Lunch
Monday—Saturday
210 West San Francisco Street
(505) 983-9880

Tomasitas

Housed in an old Train Depot, Tomasitas is a must on your gastronomical tour of Santa Fe. There are no crayons or separate kids menus although there are a few choices for the kids on the regular menu. Don't let that stop you. The green chile is probably the best in town but beware it is hot as the sign warns when you enter the restaurant. It is loud and crowded so the kids can do as they please. Try to get a table on the patio. If you have to wait for your table, which is usually the case, take a stroll over to the Santa Fe Southern Railway station across the parking lot, you may just see a train pulling out.

Lunch and Dinner
Monday—Saturday
500 South Guadalupe
(505) 983-5721

Tortilla Flats

There's nothing fancy about this family-friendly Cerillos Road restaurant, but you can always expect a good meal at a good price. Breakfast doesn't get much better than this. For mom and dad, the omelettes are delicious, especially with chorizo. For kids, the Los Ninos Special consists of two fluffy pancakes, bacon or an egg ($3.69). El Cabellero is an egg, bacon, and toast or tortilla. The food's fresh, the servings large and the booths soft and comfortable. Plus, this could be the best hot chocolate in town...complete with a big dollop of whipped cream on top.

At lunch and dinner they offer a variety of New Mexican dishes. The kids love the taco plate, bean and cheese burrito and burger and fries. Service is usually fast and good. Weekend mornings are usually busy. The place is big and there's rarely a wait. Bottom Line, if you find yourself on Cerillos Road headed to Villa Linda Mall or Jackalope, this is a good, solid place filled with locals.

Breakfast, Lunch and Dinner
Open 7 Days
3139 Cerillos Road
(505) 471-8685

Upper Crust Pizza

Eventually someone is going to beg for pizza, it has to happen. This place has been around since 1979 and continues to be a favorite of locals and visitors. All the regular toppings are here but you can also get green chile on your pie. Where else but Santa Fe? They also have salads, subs and calzones. There are two patios, one in the back and one in the front. The location can't be beat, it is right next to the San Miguel Mission and right around the corner from the Oldest House.

Lunch and Dinner
Open 7 Days
329 Old Santa Fe Trail
(505) 982-0000

Zia Diner

Is it time for a little comfort food? Well, head over to the Zia Diner. Here you will find meatloaf, turkey, hamburgers, sandwiches, salads and pasta dishes. They have a comfort food kid's menu as well and they will greet your cuties with a can o' crayons and a couple of coloring pages. But the best part has to be the soda fountain. Doesn't everyone love a milk shake with dinner? Or maybe a root beer float. The "diner" is very family oriented and your gang will fit right in. Your kids will thank you.

Breakfast, Lunch and Dinner
Open 7 Days
326 South Guadalupe
(505) 988-7008

ANNUAL CALENDAR OF EVENTS

January

Santa Fe Ski Basin Open
Turtle Dance, Taos Pueblo
Feast Days, San Ildefonso Pueblo

February

Santa Fe Ski Basin Open
Deer Dance, San Juan Pueblo

March

Santa Fe Ski Basin Open

April

Santa Fe Ski Basin Closes
Easter Dances and Celebrations, Most Pueblos

May

Santa Cruz Feast Day, Taos Pueblo

June

Santa Fe Rodeo
Santa Fe Plaza Arts and Crafts Festival
San Antonio Feast Day, Most Pueblos
Spring Festival and Animal Fair, El Rancho de las Golandrinas

July

4th of July Pancake Breakfast on the Plaza
International Folk Art Market, Milner Plaza - Museum Hill
Summer Spanish Market, The Plaza
Music at the Plaza Pavilion
Santa Fe Opera
Santa Fe Chamber Music Festival
Santa Fe Desert Chorale
Wine Festival, El Rancho de las Golandrinas
Eight Northern Pueblos Artist and Craftsman Show, San Juan Puebelo

August

Indian Market, The Plaza
Music at the Plaza Pavilion
Santa Fe Opera
Santa Fe Chamber Music Festival
Santa Fe Desert Chorale
Summer Festival, El Rancho de las Golandrinas
Santa Fe County Fair
Girls, Inc. Arts and Crafts Fair, The Plaza
Santa Clara Feast Day, Santa Clara Pueblo

September

Santa Fe Fiesta/Zozobra
Wine and Chile Festival
Feast of San Geronimo, Taos

October

Balloon Fest, Albuquerque
St. Francis of Assisi Feast Day, Nambe Pueblo
Harvest Festival, El Rancho de las Golandrinas

November

Santa Fe Ski Basin Opens
San Diego Feast Day, Tesuque Pueblo

December

Santa Fe Ski Basin Open
Winter Spanish Market, Sweeney Center
Nuestra Senora de Guadalupe Feast Day, Pojoaque, Santa Clara,
    and Tesuque Pueblos
Las Posadas, The Plaza
Christmas Celebrations, Most Pueblos

INDEX

Printed in the United States
54495LVS00007B/157-186